50 + 2 Poems Just for You

Joseph Cashman

ISBN 978-1-915502-46-9 © 2023 Joseph Cashman

All rights reserved. No part of this book may be reproduced, stored in a retrieval system, or transmitted by any means, electronic, mechanical, photocopying, recording or otherwise without written permission from the author. Published in Ireland by Orla Kelly Publishing. Cover image by the author.

Orla Kelly Publishing
27 Kilbrody,
Mount Oval,
Rochestown,
Cork,
Ireland.

This book is dedicated to my family

Acknowledgments

It is with deep gratitude that I have an opportunity to thank all who contributed directly and indirectly to bringing the poems in this book to print.

I offer my sincere thanks to Susan, Janet, Linda and my family. All, including the publisher have helped in their own unique way to place the book in your hands. This publication is a cooperative creation with a special word of thanks to Susan for her unwavering support and love of poetry.

About the Author

Joseph lives in County Waterford and enjoys walks in nature, sports of all kind and writing. Many of the poems in this book are inspired by the beautiful surrounding local areas and his family.

Contents

Acknowledgments iv
About the Author v
Listening 1
A time to face love out 2
Emissary 3
Moonlight 4
The Winding Road 5
Carefree Abandon 6
Windmill Way 8
Morning 9
Forever 10
Love's Connection 11
To Search 12
Meadow's Walk 14
Tomorrow 16
Eternal Day 17
Softly 18
Promise 19
Love Calls 20
Signs 22
When Day is Done 23
Train 24
Periphery 25
The path of least resistance 26
Where chance beckons 27
The Wonder of it all 28
Swiftness 29
Happenstance 30

Boldness of Being 32
The Hearts That Cross 33
Where faith may dwell 34
The Wings of Faith 35
Where grows the wild 36
Love's Enduring Call 37
Transformation 38
Imminent 40
Vision 42
Where willows grow 43
Ode to Love 44
Rivers of Love 46
Hope 47
The Path Beyond 48
Dawn of Day 50
Cascade 51
Tree 52
Boat Together 54
The Gift Within 56
Where Toll the Bells 57
The Gift of Presence 58
Where Beauty Grows 59
Doorways to another 60
Journey of a man 62
Serendipity 64
Homecoming 65
Please Review 66
Other Books by the Author 67

Listening

The scatter of the rustling leaves
Intruded on the forest's breathing.
Did it hop? Or…did it stop?
A thought transfixed
Upon the action of a thought.

Do rustling sounds still our minds
To beat in harmony with our hearts
Will the rustle and the listener?
Dance in synergy or apart.

Will we give time the time
To listen to our heart's desire?
Perhaps
Through listening truly.

A time to face love out

And fill my heart unendingly
With sheets of love returned,
Wafting like the summer rain
Across a verdant landscape
That felt the kiss of the morning dew.

A time to face love out
And fill my soul unendingly
Like a sun-drenched rain-filled flower
Opening its heart to nature's promise.

A simple touch, a knowing gesture,
A helping hand, a silent gift
Can bridge infinity in a single moment,
And leave the giver and the given
Blessed to overflowing.

As love faced out.

Emissary

Since the dawn of time we slumber
Through the ticking of the clock
That encloses our thought reality.
Nothing is as it seems
As yesterday's floating memory
Becomes tomorrow's dream.
We plan the fragile future
In hope of a solid present.

Can we justify our slumber
When we clean the glass of time?
To see more clearly
Our future and our present.
Habitually patterns solidify
That keep our peace of mind entangled.
Unable to break free
To hear the voice of reason beckon,
And miss the space between the words
To let the message through.

Moonlight

Across the fertile valley,
That flows into the lowly hills.
Moonlight reflects the magic
From a clear and starry sky.

And nothing goes unnoticed
As the dancing light
Bedecked with fairie stardust
Reflects upon the fragrant grassy knoll;
And fireflies weave in unison,
Under the blossoming lilac tree.

While nature's friendly creatures
Playfully leave their prints
Upon the verdant slopes,
As the night-calls
Of passing vixen and fleeting hare,
Echoes their journey,
Through the dappled, dancing light.

The Winding Road

Many a footprint
Covers the winding road
With an imprint of sureness
That is marked by faith.

And many a path is widened
By those that stumble
And those that follow
On their next step of discovery.

To gift the follower
With a sure and steady step
And take them onwards
Towards a new and vibrant place.

How many wayward travellers
Step on the uncharted path
And leave an imprint
As imperceptible as the wind
That flutters the willow leaf.

Leaving the winding road
A safer place to wander
And give hope along the way.

Carefree Abandon

Can the butterfly flap its wings
In carefree abandon?
If the caterpillar never shed its cocoon?
Can the wind spread its wings
Upon the sea and clouds?
If it never made the journey there;
Would the wind and sea miss the clouds?
If the droplets never rose
To grace the sky with glee
And fall to feed the rose?

Can we ever fathom the unfathomable
From a single vantage point?
If we ever made it there
Would we be secure in knowing
How the waves caressed the shores
And threw the sand about
With carefree reckless abandon?
Or see the seagull jump the waves
And rest upon its pulsing throb,
Can we ever meet the maker
Who flames the beauty that never ceases
To shine the magic laden imprint
On carefree abandon?

Windmill Way

Throughout the rolling hills
And sprawling cornfields
Windmill way tends
To its maker's task.

As barges, horse and cart
Make their weary way
Along well-trodden paths
To windmills, waiting to be fed.

And geese busily chase
The falling grains of corn
That drip from the leaking corners
Of the trundling laden carts.

Noisily the children play
In nearby swaying reeds
And chase the nesting water hen,
Who scatters to the water's edge
Out of reach of childish hands
Down busy windmill way.

Morning

In the undulating rippling water
Upon the silent lakeside shore
Buffeted by the soft wind of morning
Floats a shimmering surface,
Bereft of tidal flow.

A seagull calls to its mate
And listens for reply
As they ready to begin their journey
To furthest land and shore.

And from the beckoning call
An echoing reply pours forth
Ringing along the shoreline
From ears that heard,
And heart that listened.

To a sound long familiar
That brings their wings to one another
To flap in unison upon the open skies
Above the rolling waves far below
To find their home amongst the dunes
With family and a fertile foam.

Forever

The sigh of evening seals the end of day
And wraps its warm summer's coat
Around the forming of the dewdrop
That hangs by a silver spider's thread
As breaking dawn approaches.

Are there many mornings
That herald the rising dawn?
To hang its nascent tapestry
Upon forever's presence,
Silently waiting to add another day
To the fleeting calendar?

Can it be that simple,
To forever's courteous call
That all our days
Lie on the fringes of forever?

While children imagine in the moment
In pure joy, unexplained
To play on the fringes of forever
And never miss a beat
A pulse in
Forever's memory.

Love's Connection

Love's connection hangs like a ripened fruit
Waiting for a gentle touch
To place it in the outstretched hand.
Slowly gathering its maker's gift
With gentle caress and steady purpose.
And place its bounty in a sure and safe place.

Naught is missing or wasted in this blossoming space
As love's gentle connection gathers pace
A fragile fragrance crosses the threshold of belief
Like a slumbering ember
That catches the welcoming wind
And sparks anew with sweeping hope.
To lie in the land of plenty
And never falter.

To Search

    Is central to our being.
        Perhaps,
            That is why we are here
                In this moment of time.

Life

    Is a journey
        Of many experiences
            And myriad paths
            To walk upon.
                That journey through
                    The outer landscapes
                      Spanning the vistas
                      Before our eyes.

Learning

    To love oneself
        May be the greatest journey,
            Of them all.

From here

All rivers
    Flow homewards
        Through the inner realms
        To our divinity.
           That link the bridges
          Between
              Our heart and soul
              And nurture us
                Unendingly.

Meadow's Walk

Down by the meadow's walk
That weaves through dale and glen,
The quiet hum of busy bees
Breaks the silence there.

As dust swirls in the air
O'er wafts of spinning wind
To lazily land adrift,
In nearby pastures green.

Ladybirds gather nearby
To regale the sun-drenched path
And open their coloured shells
In the leafy hollow glen.

How does the meadow
Weave its canopy
Over the carefree dell
For all who visit there.

And would those who saunter there
Bestow a fleeting glance
At the wonder of it all,
And lift the silence
Through their very
Presence there?

Tomorrow

Can the joy be felt
In tomorrow's silent call
That floats across
Horizon's furthest line.

And float with ephemeral ease
Through the corners of our mind.
To catch a moment's call
That lies within tomorrow's reach.

As it silently lays
In its special waiting place
To be found when called upon
And expressed
In myriad ways.

Eternal Day

We light the lamp to find our way
On the journey forth in life
And bless the many gifts
Our light illuminates.

As each passing season
Becomes a year
Adding to and growing the light
A little more.

To shine upon our heart's longings
And gently guide us to,
The gateway of eternal day
That sees the light in everyone.

Softly

In the cloud-speckled sky
Softly billowing with the wind
The light dances between
The carefree birds
That fly around beneath;

And the light breath of evening
Stills the scudding clouds
As the morning rain
Invites the sun
To return again.

The carefree touch
Of the meadow
Brings its morning smell of freshness
And all is blended as one
As the sun shines again.

Promise

The pestle smooths the stubborn clay
And with the finest stroke
The artist gently coaxes
And blends anew
A palette of chosen pigments
To grace the canvas and our lives.

And the brush strokes
Tell their story
On canvas newly stretched
As the vibrant colours mixed
Fill in the detail in between
Breathing promise into form
With colours that adorn
The promise of something new.

Love Calls

Where trust is born
Hope and faith skims the surface
Of our chosen thoughts.

And calls between the doubts and fears
To glisten anew as a morning dewdrop
On the narrow path of its domain;
Where joy and trust are polished afresh
With sombre promise of fidelity blessed.

That build the bridges of trust today
To span the high tides of tomorrow
And lay a path of faith along the way,
For a sure and steady step
Upon the stepping stones of hope.

Where love calls to hands that hold
The dreams and vision of two hearts
To beat as one upon the dreams of today
And share the vision,
Sitting on the horizons of tomorrow.

Signs

A falling feather, a fluttering leaf
A happenstance meeting
Can bring joy into the smallest detail
Of our lives.

And expectant anticipation
Into the space between
Grace and hope,
That flows serendipitously
On the edges of our lives.

While many a sign arriving unannounced
Lifts and flutters the imagination
And blesses the road of things to come

Where faith and hope
Can nourish the tiniest seed
And blend the magic and the reason
As one.

When Day is Done

When day is done
Night time beckons
The starlit heavens
To dance upon the fallen snow.

With velvet touch
And easy charm
That sparkles gently
As a thousand suns.

And robins chirp upon
The berry-laden holly tree
At the bounty of it all,
As the heavens alight
On the glistening path
To home.

Where light-filled windows
And open door
Welcomes the beauty
To come within,

As hands are clasped
And ushered in
With eyes and hearts
That meet as One.

Train

Through the pristine dawn
Billowing smoke wafts around
The heaving platform
Of passengers,
Going to a new and steady place,
Far from the familiar,
Where adventure and the new
Await them.

And steadily, with laden carriages
And winding tracks,
Chugging sounds and steep incline,
Train leaves the sleepy hamlet
Far below

And beckon anew,
To those that don't
Look back,
To places and names
Not yet seen or heard.

Periphery

All things pass
With fleeting promise
Of a moment blessed
With pristine newness.

How many moments
Sleep on the periphery
And corners of our mind?
To awaken when promise
Comes knocking at the door,

And how many moments
Are graced by
Serendipitous ease
To flow freely
And touch the centre of our lives?

Can it be that providence awaits
On the periphery of our lives?
Untouched by time
To blossom unfettered
With benign beauty
And imminent grace,

To promises slumbering
In heartfelt wishes
That wait expectantly
On the fringes of time.

The path of least resistance

If we could peer
Through the glass of time
To plot the course
Of life's travails
And see what others can't,

Would we be satisfied
With the course we chose?
Or wish to find another way
Halfway through…
And start again?
Or leave it all to chance?

Perhaps choose,
The path of least resistance
Where every pasture
Is newly born
Of heart's request
And live a life
That is soul fulfilled.

Where chance beckons

Where chance beckons
Water will take the effortless path,
Sweeping around
The rock and eddy
To make its journey
To the sea.

And eagles soar
To float upon
The rising air,
Climbing the stairway
Of heaven's calling
To flap the wings
No more than needed.

As roses blossom
When the time is right
To face the sun and bees alike
And surrender all
To nature's calling.

The Wonder of it all

Do we ever ponder
What fills the space
Between the word and the thought?
Before the sound
Crosses the threshold
Of our lips.

Or ever wonder
What causes the apple to fall?
In the still air
Of harvest time?

Can we ever fathom
What brings
The thought to form?

Or can all be surrendered
Free of fettered thoughts,
To fill our world
With the wonder of it all.

Swiftness

The grace parlayed to those that dare
To ask the way that is not defined.

Step outside the bounds of time
And touch the boundless through courage,
Without demand.

To free the way with exquisite swiftness
Of unfolding grace,
Along the path that measures the miracle
Within each moment in time,

From the doorway and between the worlds
That gently open wide.

Happenstance

A thousand spores
From laden dandelion flowers,
Waft lazily
O'er the summer fields.

And land where may
And wafts of wind allow,
Or rise again in happenstance
To seek more fertile ground.

And life wraps
Its benign coat
Around the onward journey
Where every breath of wind
Reminds

That all is remembered
And all is possible
To begin anew.

Boldness of Being

The caterpillar dares to dream
Of life beyond the cocoon shell
That hangs by a silver thread
From a doorway
To another world.

And life surrenders all
To make the dream come true
Gently pouring its love
Upon the shell
To bless the caterpillar's
Boldness of being.

Slowly the dream surrenders
To life's incessant call
That unlocks the shell's reality
And pathways to the skies.

To boldly become
The butterfly it is meant to be
And spread it's silken wings
Upon the open skies
To embrace a life renewed.

The Hearts That Cross

Like waves that wash
Against the incoming stream
That makes the journey home to sea,
From the clear and bubbling mountain source
Springing forth high above the valley floor
And mountain flora blooming far below.

Where flocks of sheep busily graze verdant slopes
Besides the now cascading, rushing stream
And quench their thirst in its riverside eddies
As the setting sun sets the sea ablaze,
With ever changing liquid, shimmering hues.

Gently the stream journeys onward
Through vales of plenty and fertile woodlands
As the stream's calm and sky-filled waters
Of lazily drifting puffy clouds,
Reflect upon its golden light-filled bed.

While families and their loved ones meet
To bask upon its blooming summer banks
And bathe in the welcoming depths
As waves wash upon the nearby shoreline.

So the hearts that cross flow gently
Homeward to each other
May they never waver from the flow within
And then meet to merge at journey's end.

Where faith may dwell

Like a beacon
From a distant shoreline
Faith shines its light
When it seems least needed.

It alights upon the planted seed
That holds the promise within its core
To be all that which it can be.

And awaits upon that expectant moment
Where faith may dwell with benign care
Upon the emergent seedling's tender shoot.
There to grace its every movement
With a blessed ease of unfolding grace
Where every reach of seedling towards the light
Is marked by the turning of its world.

That welcomes the rising dawn
Sweeping across the morning sky
Beckoning it's leaves to unfold
Until rest beneath the starlight
As faith dreams the dream in unison
With the tender shoot's heartfelt wishes
On its journey to completion.

The Wings of Faith

The wings of faith
Bestows the All
In Loving Grace,
And spreads
Its mighty hand,
Across land and foam.

And never doubts
The graced terrain,
Heavenward prayers
That plants the seed,
To grow the vine
As it pours its goodness
From heaven's door.

Where grows the wild

Where grows the wild
Unfettered heart
Whose dreams are tossed
To the four winds.

To blossom silently
In unbroken places,
Where answers are not sought
Or given,
To till the soil
And share the dream

With hearts that know
The dream is real.

Love's Enduring Call

From the whispering
Corridors of time,
Love's enduring call
Echoes on forever
From Heaven's heart,

And washes over everything
To find a home
In every heart
To return the call
With every beat.

Transformation

The thoughts that bind our fears
Are pathways to the inner realm,
Footprints through these pathways
Are only visible through our actions,
Leaving thoughts and fears behind us
On the surface of our past.

Opening channels of expression
That build bridges between the heart and mind
For creativity to bloom forth vividly
Through imagining and spoken, written word
And the fertile ground of a feeling heart.

In a language known and felt,
By the flowering emotional landscape
Blossoming effortlessly in the moment
That link the voice of reason and heart's longings
Awakening our creative gifts within.

Through freshly imagined vistas
And new lands to be journeyed to
On exploration's infinite possibilities,
Dreamed into being with pure intent
To create the blooming of a life fulfilled.

Imminent

From days and nights to the ocean's swell,
All answer to the call of time
And never step beyond its bounds.
Where every clock measures their journey
From month to month and season's end
To times of tides on every shoreline.

Never wandering from the hands of time
Who measures their movement
Across time's domain, whose gaze is set in stone.
From journeys back in memories
And forward to tomorrow's land
Counted in the second and bits too small to imagine.

And when the imminent moment arrives
Unannounced before our eyes
The gaze of time relinquishes
To an ever-present pause
That lies within the unmeasurable moment,
Between the hands of time's inhale and exhale
Unlocking the keys of time that turn
Our future and the past.

Where All is filled with infinite possibility
Within the pause of the unmeasurable moment.
Awaiting our recognition of it's feeling of familiarity

Within a quiet mind and gentle heart
That awaken gifts to blossom with pure intent
And creativity to birth our dreams and longings
From the imminent beauty ever present
When creating in the unmeasurable moment.

Vision

Where swallows lie
The ground is sown with a vision,
Of lifelong love.
As wings swoop in with graceful ease
And flight's delight from distant lands
Across the sea.

And comes ashore to a nest built
For family and fidelity.
That anchors the joy in a haven berth
And seeds the love
With graces blessed unendingly.

As wings are spread upon the skies domain
From morning until the setting sun
To nurture new life with mouths to feed
Awaiting at the threshold of their nest
For nature's gifts from parents' beaks.

That take no count or score
Of chores shared
Or gaze at other for the sake of charm.
They remain as one,
To turn the pages with each other.

Where willows grow

Where willows grow
The air is laden
With the softest hope
Of a welcome wind.

Like a lover's glance
That flutters the heart
Into remembrance
And moves the soul
Into belonging.

Ode to Love

As dolphins call
To their mate,
Their echoing sound
Wanders through
The spiralling pathway
Of the waiting seashell.

Where hands that hold
And ear that listen,
Hear the call,
In the waiting heart.

And as the call
Travels the pathways
Of the heart,
Unfolding waves
Blossom anew,
As Ode to Love
Reaches the fertile ground
Of a waiting heart.

And all is gathered
In a playful way,
Through the spirals
Of the soul
That sends the call forth
To the mirrored soul.

Rivers of Love

Rivers of love
Flow unendingly
Through every vein
To join as one
In the home of the heart,
Where all is transformed
To begin again.

And every movement
Outward
Breathes new life everywhere
As the hope of the heart,
Nourishes all.

As every river turns
It promises new love everywhere
To heart and body and soul.

And when the promises
Are all done
And dreams and yearnings are fulfilled
Each river makes its journey homeward
To reunion
Within the chambers of the heart.

Hope

Hope sits in the wind
Hovering in perfect stillness
Never knowing when called upon
To grace the centre of our being
With impeccable timing and a healing touch.

Carefree and daring
To move beyond confines of time and space,
To reach, unhindered,
The most unlikely space and place
Never stretching past the invite
Yet forever ready
To be
The invited guest.

The Path Beyond

In a little island oasis,
The path beyond
Our beating heart
Dwells in love
And holds a space
For every beat.

And many a road
May take us there
Oft' times in roundabout ways,
To where the mirrored heart
Resides in fullness
In the soul's longings.

And from this place,
The call goes out
To every road
That leads us there.

And time stands still,
In this same place
With no bells to toll
For end of day.

As all is possible
In this welcome space
Where doors are open
And windows wide
To see within
And venture there.

Dawn of Day

With exultant joy
The cockerel crows at dawn of day
And calls upon the heaven's light
To descend from the firmament.

As lighter clothes and brighter colours
Are draped across the bedside edge
Beneath sunlight's warm soothing rays,
To announce the passing of the night.

And bathroom windows flung open wide
Welcome the warmth of the day
As fresh pure air is ushered in
Inviting the breath to draw the fragrance
Of the morning gently in.

While cockerel stands upon the window ledge
To watch the heaven's pour from outside in
And call upon his family,
To greet the day and morning's light.

Cascade

They fly together in heaven's skies
With grace and beauty of eagle wings
And never wander far from one another,
As outstretched wings surveys all.

And as they turn the light cascades
From underwing to earth's domain
And bless the ground beneath their feet
As they climb again a little more
On circular stairways of rising air
Calling across the cloud speckled sky
That echoes along the valley far below
They climb to touch the clouds.

When the journeys of the day are done
And the stairways of heaven's skies
Are soared to hearts content
Wings are folded in restful poise
Beside their nest with vistas wide
High up on the woodside slopes.

That watches all beneath their gaze
Across the verdant tree-filled valley,
Stretching out before their resting eyes
Where rolling hills of blooming heather
Reach up to the mountainside
As the sun's bright rays slide below,
The furthest land on horizon's shore.

Tree

From fertile valley
To mountain side
Tree stands majestic
Upon it all
And reaches heavenward
To the Light.

While all around
Nature's guests
Bring their babies home,
To nest and rest.

As deepest root
Draws its nourishment
Within
To build its strength
And growth alike.

And when the summer days
Are spent
Rustic leaves adorn her coat
And float in time,
Beneath her feet
With blessed gifts
For passing squirrel.

As fleeting days
And longer nights

Find their way into season
Branch-filled tree
Sweep across the landscape.

And turn its gaze
Upon the skies,
To be the sentinel
Of the starlight.

Boat Together

Where rushes grow
And sunflowers sway together
Where water ripples
And breezes play
Between the reeds.

Lovers are cast
By knowing hands
From landing place
To water's edge,
Where outstretched oars
And each oar splash
Guides the boats that journey forth,

And reflections
Mirror all around
Upon the waters
And boat alike
As oar, water and boat
Become one with each other.

With every movement
A new wish is born
To make the journey
In the boat together
To places not yet seen
Or discovered
And when the journey

Is complete
And all the wishes are fulfilled
They both return
To landing place
Where helpful hands
Guide them back,
To solid ground once more.

The Gift Within

The gift within is a many facet gem
That alights from inspiration's door
And travels in the moment
To rest upon the heart's terrain
With pure intent and positivity;

As it creates upon the energies
Ebbing and flowing gently,
On the rich emotional shores
Igniting the emotional vistas
That span the solid, subtle and sublime.

Where joy and heartfelt wishes
Unfolds the awaiting imagination
To blossom in the synergy
Of heart, mind and oft' times Soul
Through feelings, senses and subtle signs too
Softly awakening our creating gift within.

To create through word and deed with pure intent
And sometimes recreate what is already there
Or play within our awakened, creating gift
With infinite ingenuity and free expression
Where reflections of the unfolding creation,
Births effortlessly into form before our eyes
Fulfilling the whispered wishes of the gift within.

Where Toll the Bells

Where toll the bells
The deepest sea
Ushers shallow waters
In between
The towering headlands
And hidden reefs.

Like two lovers
Singing upon the waters
Their pillars of sound
Reach out across the sea
And wrap around
The sailors' journey home.

To bring their gifts
And laden treasures
In to safe haven
And sharing space
With those who seek
Their bounty there.

The Gift of Presence

With impeccable grace
The gift of presence
Gathers all to itself,
Aligned with Love,

And sees the sublime
In everything
While never measuring
Anything,
As all is blessed
At the feet of Love,

That pours its gift
Upon the presence
Of the moment
To touch the quiet mind
With gentle ease.

While the receptive heart
Catches the gentle breeze
Of a moment blessed,
With fleeting promise
And pristine newness
Upon the pathway of today.

Where Beauty Grows

Where beauty grows
The grass is wild
And never tended to,
As flowers frolic
To their heart's content
Between the grass and shade.

And butterflies land
Where beauty lies
Between the grass
And outstretched flowers
To spread their wings
Of wonder
Upon the warm earth.

And nothing matters
Where time is lost
In nature's open heart
And soothing charm.

Awakening all under sun's bright light
From morning dew until evening calm
To blossom beauty unsurpassed
Till day is spent and night calls,
Radiant flowers of every hue
To close their petal coats
For sleep beneath the stars.

Doorways to another

Easy gaze upon the rose
Unfolds the petals of the heart
That sees the beauty in everything.
And mirrors form all around
That gift more beauty to behold,
And opens doorways everywhere
To see the beauty in another.

Where from this place,
In heart's domain
Our gifts are shared
With no measure taken there
Of what remains to hoard or grasp;
Completing the circle
That nurtures receiving and giving
From doorways to another.

To bless the beauty in our lives
Of sharing gifts with pure intent
From the simple to profound
That sees the joy in others eyes
And seeds the ground beneath their feet
With infinite possibility and surprise
Creating hope and much, much more
Along the pathways of tomorrow.

Journey of a man

From the first breath
The journey of a man
Begins to unfold
Upon life's many paths
Some tried and tested
And other yet not trodden
That beckons him to adventures new.

And many journeys too
Spring from
The cradle of his guardian's arms
From the first step
To ventures far from home
And many things are put aside
As childhood yields
To adolescence ways.

And when adolescent days are spent
New horizons come afresh
As memories and melodies
Are put aside once more.

To sail upon the seas of life
Where every rudder turn
Is guided by his hand
On journeys often planned
And sometimes left to happenstance.

While journeys new
Are shared with one other too
To bless his life
With ventures new
And new lands to journey to.

Serendipity

From the hand
That rests softly
On the folded page
Whose crease was made
With a benign touch.

So, too, serendipity
Rests with easy lay
Upon tomorrow's
Present moment
That falls gracefully
Into the open heart,
And unfolds in life
As roses bloom.

Homecoming

As the golden soil
Sweeps beneath the rose
And comes ashore
On the grassy verge,
The crystal-laden
Grass-filled dewdrops
Shine forth their light
Upon the shore
With brilliant hue.

And every blade of grass
Bows down to meet
The journey home
Of a golden friend,
That reaches up
Its golden hand
To light the path
Between them.

And every door
Is open wide
To usher in
Their homecoming.

Please Review

Dear reader,

I hope you enjoyed my collection of poems '50+2 Just for You.' It would be most appreciated if you could spread the word so others may find my poetry and also if you can leave a review if you bought the book online.

Thank you.

Joseph

Other Books by the Author

Family and Love Poems is an uplifting and inspiring collection of poetry that celebrates the beauty of family and love. Richly illustrated and offering an array of positive insights, readers will be taken on an emotional journey full of meaningful moments.

Through this book, you will explore the special place family holds in our lives, the joys of love, the blessings of relationships, and more.

Each poem is overflowing with colourful imagery and heartwarming emotions. Not only will it touch the heart, but also inspire curiosity and invite you to reflect on the many facets of love.

Let this book be your guide to discovering all that life has to offer and truly appreciate its joys and depths. Find solace in the words of Family and Love Poems and create lasting memories to cherish for a lifetime.

DIVINE DESIGN Poetry of the Heart and Soul is a sublime collection of poetry that speaks to the heart and soul. Uncovering the special relationship between the heart, soul and Divine with deep understanding and scintillating clarity. Each poem is a treasure trove of beautiful moments and a freshness that is exhilarating, encouraging us to recognise Divine Design all around us.

Many of the poems in this anthology are filled with wonderful insights taking the reader on a journey of discovery. Moments such as simple acts of sharing with those we love, friends who help us out, or when paths cross just by chance--show that we are always cared for and loved. They also speak of Divine Design soaring over Earth below to bless teeming seas and shores with shoals of fish and fertile waters as well as nature's gardens and landscapes and all creatures who dwell there.

Finally, the book reminds us that our Creator's infinite light and love blesses Earth, all life, and humanity endlessly -- something we can certainly aspire to do ourselves in our daily lives.

This book is perfect for readers wanting to explore how their own lives are blessed through Divine Design. Through its thoughtful writing and exquisite illustrations, readers can share moments of joy, love, abundance, and kindness as they delve into the mysterious depths of Divine Design.

So come and enjoy a journey of heart and soul in this beautiful book of poetry.

www.ingramcontent.com/pod-product-compliance
Lightning Source LLC
Chambersburg PA
CBHW041309110526
44590CB00028B/4306